Moon Project

Written by Rachel Blackman
Created by the Company

Published by Playdead Press 2013

© Rachel Blackman

Rachel Blackman has asserted her rights under the Copyright, Design and Patents Act, 1988, to be identified as the author of this work.

A CIP catalogue record for this book is available from the British Library.

ISBN 978-1-910067-02-4

Caution
All rights whatsoever in this play are strictly reserved and application for performance should be sought through the author before rehearsals begin. No performance may be given unless a license has been obtained.

This book is sold subject to the condition that it shall not by way of trade or otherwise, be lent, resold, hired out, or otherwise circulated without the publisher's prior consent in any form of binding or cover other than that in which it is published and without a similar condition including this condition being imposed on the subsequent purchaser.

Printed by BPUK

Playdead Press
www.playdeadpress.com

This script was correct at the time of printing and is based on a version of the work created by the company, who at the time of writing included: Performers; Rachel Blackman and Jules Munns, Directors; Paul Hodson (including dramaturgy) and Emma Roberts (including movement direction), Lighting and Production Management; Greg Mickelborough, Sound Design by the Company, Costume and Set Design; Pearl Bates, Stage Management; Lloyd Thomas and Producer Beccy Smith.

This version of Moon Project was produced by Ovalhouse London, with the generous support of Bradford's Theatre in The Mill, South Street Arts Reading and The Nightingale. Moon Project was supported with funds provided by Arts Council England.

THE COMPANY

Rachel Blackman (writer / performer) is a theatre maker, actress, writer and producer. She trained and worked as an actress in Australia before relocating to the UK where she is now based. As Artistic Director of Stillpoint, she has created four full length works including three award winning solo plays: *The Art of Catastrophe; Steal Compass, Drive North, Disappear* and *The Growing Room*. Together they comprise: *Triptych: Three Attempts at Love*. In 2012 Rachel received commissions to create two shorter works. One for Fuel Theatre's Phenomenal People and the other by The Nightingale to create *The Department of Unreliable Memoirs* with Emma Kilbey. She is also one half of the ongoing two woman improvised play Katy and Rach.

Moon Project is Rachel's fourth full length work and the first for two performers. It was created with a commission from Ovalhouse and the assistance of Arts Council England. It was also generously supported by Bradford's Theatre in the Mill, South Street Reading and The Nightingale.

Paul Hodson (co-director) has worked in theatre as a writer, dramaturg and director for 30 years, starting as Director of Nightingale Theatre, Brighton. He has also written over 100 hours of broadcast TV, but is feeling better now. Theatre shows include adapting and directing *Fever Pitch*. Original writing includes Edinburgh Fringe First winning Meeting *Joe Strummer, Way Out West* and *Brighton 'Til I Die*, all for The Future Is Unwritten. In 2013 he has directed *Garage Band* by Andy Barrett at Mercury Theatre, Colchester and Dramaturged Victoria Melody's *Major Tom*. He is currently making a piece about Englishness, *England Away*, for national tour 2014.

Emma Roberts (co-director) currently works as a movement director, director and educator in movement studies. She works in the UK and France teaching somatic improvisation and embodiment practices. She is a founder member of Stillpoint Theatre and was the co-creator and director of the company's first ever show *The Art of Catastrophe*. Emma also runs her own company, Shaping the Invisible, which focuses on collaboration and education in all areas of the community. Previous to her current practice, Emma worked as an actress, including in *Persuasion* (BBC film 1995), the lead in TV Series *Revelations, Crime Time* (Film 1997), as well as various other TV and theatre. She has also performed extensively as an improviser with Shaping the Invisible.

Jules Munns (performer) is a producer, director and performer based in London. He performs with improvisation company the Maydays and is one half of Ten Thousand Million Love Stories, an improvised love story, which is touring the UK in 2014. He has also performed with Music Box - The Improvised Musical and the Improsarios and is the director of Impromptu Shakespeare. He is the founder of Slapdash International, London's longest running festival of improvisation and one of the directors of the Nursery, a space in Southwark devoted to new theatre and improvisation. He trained at the Guildhall school.

Pearl Bates (designer) studied theatre design at Central Saint Martin's College of Art & Design before going on to forge a career as a fine artist. Described as 'Schiele goes fashion', Pearl Bates' paintings have been exhibited internationally and feature in two books. She fuses together a diverse range of inspirations such as haut couture, street culture, music, film, dance, architecture and the natural environment, and uses paint, ink, pencil and collage to explore the hidden, magical dimensions of real people who have captured the artist's imagination. Three years ago, a chance opportunity in the wardrobe department at Glyndebourne Opera House drew Bates back into the world of theatre and performance, and *Moon Project* is her first professional theatre design commission.

Lloyd Thomas (stage manager) studied in Music Production and Technology in Coventry, later taking this to Degree level at Northbrook College, Worthing. He began working freelance in 2003 as a sound and lighting technician at various venues and theatres in Brighton.

Credits include; Gravity and Levity's *Shift*, sound operation, Ragroof Theatre *Gloves On*, SM LX and sound op and The Future is Unwritten's *Fever Pitch*, SM and LX/sound op. Other projects include FOH sound and tour management for bands 'Moulettes' and 'The Crazy World of Arthur Brown'. He also works closely with Acute Audio Production of Brighton.

Greg Mickelborough (lighting design, production manager) is a freelance production manager and lighting designer who has toured extensively in the UK and abroad with artists including The Two Wrongies (World of Wrong), Victoria Melody (Northern Soul; Major Tom), aerial theatre company BandBazi (Mind Walking), 30 Bird Productions (Chodzine-Siberia; Domestic Labour), Bryony Kimmings (Seven Day Drunk), Ragroof Theatre (Shall We Dance: Encore!; Bridges y Puentes), and Spymonkey (Spookshow). Greg was Production Manager for the award winning Brighton Fringe 2012 theatrical event Dip Your Toe, and has worked as venue and technical manager of The Basement and the Nightingale theatres. Greg is also the Production Manager of Festibelly music festival, and is currently part of the team converting Brighton's St Marks Chapel into a new theatrical art centre and creation space. www.gregmick.co.uk

Beccy Smith (producer) is a freelance producer and dramaturg focussing on the development of new original work for theatre. Recent freelance projects include producing *Somnmabules & the & Deadly Sins* (Karavan Ensemble, Summerhall, Edinburgh), producing Punched, a regular night of new puppetry for grown ups in Brighton and dramaturgy for *The Messenger* (Limbik Theatre), and *This Way Up* (Theatre Lark). Beccy runs visual theatre company TouchedTheatre from their base in Brighton, who in 2013 have created interactive puppetry production Blue and a national tour of dance-puppetry duet, *Headcase*. She also co-runs youth arts organisation Cultures Club, based in East Brighton and teaches regularly at Goldsmiths and Kingston Universities. Beccy is the Reviews Editor of Total Theatre magazine.

Anti-heroes and underdogs.
Stories told sideways.
The things under the bed.
Theatre for people with something to say.
New work for new audiences.

Since the 1960s, Ovalhouse has been a pioneering supporter of queer, feminist and diverse performance work. We remain committed to challenging preconceptions of what theatre is and can be.

Ovalhouse's current programme embodies our commitment to true artistic diversity, our appetite for experimentation with form and our dedication to process.

ovalhouse.com | @ovalhouse

Ovalhouse Theatre

Directors of Theatre: **Rebecca Atkinson-Lord & Rachel Briscoe**
Producer: **Faith Dodkins**
Theatre Manager: **Aaron Lamont**
Technical Manager: **Pablo Fernandez-Baz**

Front of House
Box Office Coordinator: **Alex Clarke**
Front of House Assistants: **Ros Bird, Tex Vincent Bishop, Justin Chinyere, Lorren Comert, Amirah Garba, Soniya Kapur, Michael Salami, Shavani Seth, Bevan Vincent, Emily Wallis**

Marketing
Head of Press & Marketing: **Debbie Vannozzi**
Press & Marketing Assistant: **Amelia De-Felice**

Development
Head of Fundraising: **Martyn Holland**
Fundraiser: **Julia Calver**

Ovalhouse
52-54 Kennington Oval
London
SE11 5SW
Tel: 020 7582 0080
Box Office: 020 7582 7680
Fax: 020 7820 0990
info@ovalhouse.com

Executive
Director: **Deborah Bestwick**
General Manager: **Wendy Dempsey**

Participation
Director of Participation: **Stella Barnes**
Head of Youth Arts: **Toby Clarke**
Truth About Youth Creative Producer: **Ruth Hawkins**
Head of Arts Inclusion: **Emily Doherty**
Creative Youth Inclusion Coordinator: **Lara Stavrinou**
Arts Education Assistant: **Cat Lee**
Pastoral Care and Monitoring: **Jeanie Reid**

Administration
Finance Manager: **Tony Ishiekwene**
Administrative Manager: **Annika Brown**
Archivist: **Rabyah Manzoor**

Board
Martin Humphries, Chair
Merle Campbell, Deputy Chair
Mike Bright, Treasurer
Graham Wiffen, Company Secretary
Oladipo Agboluaje
Mat Fraser
Esther Leeves
Robin Priest
John Spall
Brian Walters

Actor:
SHAHAB: *A middle aged man of American / Iranian descent living in Britain.*
JULIE: *An 25 year old Australian female sports instructor.*

Actress:
LEILA: *A middle aged British woman of mixed parentage living in Britain.*
ANJA: *A Polish/ British writer in her early thirties.*

ACT 1
Britain. The present.

SCENE 1

Pre-show lights and music. Preshow music ends. After clearance is given, Metronomy's The Look (or something with a similar function) plays as if pre-show.
House lights fade and music continues over.
And first lighting state slowly fades up.
Bob Fosse style up-beat dance routine introducing the figures of Leila and Shahab in comic relief
Music fades into radio (from inside Shahab's car).
Radio continues, then suddenly the sound of screeching brakes.
Lights snap up on two figures.
The moment before impact.
Then a woman's body is smashed across the windscreen of a man's car, with an horrific thud.
Snap to black.
Little bit more radio which fades out as a car drives off.
Silence.

SCENE 2

LX

SFX *Happiness, Jonsi & Alex (or something similar)*

A light dawns on the face of a man (Shahab) who is looking at a distant horizon. His gaze gradually expands to take in the space around him as does the light.

The sky gradually opens up to reveal an astral plane full of stars.

Then his hands are drawn upwards very gradually as if filled with helium. He tries to pull one downwards, which retracts like a snail's antennae being touched. Briefly. But then it is pulled up again in spite of him. His eyes can only focus from the horizon up. This sequence continues over -

A woman enters (Leila). She is trying to respond to all the tasks she expects of herself. She goes here and there and has to be there before she has even properly arrived here. It is as if she is on a monocycle that can never be allowed to stop incase she topples over. She must be in constant motion. Her feet beat a rhythm out on the floor as she walks / cycles and the rhythm gradually accelerates as pressure on her mounts until she is reduced to hovering / wheeling over a tiny point. She can move in angles, straight lines and points that wheel around the corners. Her eyes can only focus from the horizon down.

The two are not aware of each other, yet somehow, as she compacts, Shahab is set free to spin.

Then the cycle repeats. Only this time, Shahab is beginning to lose helium from his hands and fingers and head, whilst Leila begins muttering the following to herself. She is barely audible.

LEILA: (*muttering*)
5.30am...
6.00am (prepare breakfast. Feed Dad breakfast.)
6.45am (gather my things. All weather jacket. Trainers. Helmet.)
7.30am... *(continues through out)*

As she compacts, Shahab is some how set free to spin. The Cycle repeats. Only this time Shahab is suddenly desirous of his bed. Shahab mutters as Leila is heard clearly.

LEILA: 5.30am
wake up
wake dad
put on a load of washing
put dad in the shower, dress dad
6.00am put me in the shower, dress me
make breakfast
6.30am eat breakfast
feed dad breakfast

SHAHAB: (*muttered*) So, Tuesday.
Tuesday is,
Tuesday...
Tuesday is...

LEILA: put dad back in front of the film
6.45am Lip stick. Work shoes. Pannier bags.
6.50am greet Anne, dad's carer talk her through the day
6.55am All-weather jacket. Trainers. Helmet.
7.00am cycle to train station
park bike
buy a newspaper I won't have time to read

SHAHAB: Tereza.
Anja

LEILA: 7.19am commuter train to london
7.25am man standing so close can feel his breath in right ear.
Bollocks, didn't hang washing out. Idiot.

SHAHAB: 7am
7am.
Ok, 7 is ok
Could be a lot worse

LEILA: 8.20 Queue for coffee. Buy a coffee I won't have time to drink.
8.45am in through the doors of the natural history museum and down into the bowels.
8.50 turn on desk top. Peel the lid off the coffee that I will not drink.

8.55 pull up the days work.
9.00am my day begins.

Final cycle. Leila collects furniture for Shahab to fall into. The two characters are still in separate worlds and unaware of each other.

SHAHAB: Daylight!
Where did the night go?

Leila brings chair. Shahab constantly moving feeling own skin. Snakey / Cat-like. Has a different hand gesture for every woman.

Slipping through my fingers.

She was quite nice...
Teresa.

Shahab describes a suggestion of the waist with his hands. Leila arranges table.

I could have let her stay...
But...

Sonia stayed last week,
That was a bad idea.
It usually is a bad idea.
They think it is an invitation...

(Shahab goes to bed)

    7am.
    Ok, 7 is ok
    Could be a lot worse
    Get Iris to get the screen replaced.

Leila takes a chair and sits at the front of the stage cast downwards

    Tereza

    But Anja!
    Gossamer.
    Mysterious.
    And just when I think I have her, she vanishes!

    She might be my Diana

    Dyed hair probably.
    With eyebrows like that.

    Too awake to sleep.
    Little spiff to take the edge off.
    So Tuesday . . .
    Tuesday is . . .
    Tuesday.
    Tuesday is . . .

Anja...
Preraphaelite
40s details
She doesn't know her power.
That tiny kiss she gives me as she says goodbye
my whole heart is stolen!
Gone! Like that!

I hope she doesn't have a husband.

It is unbearable,
That I do not have her!
It is wonderful.

Tuesday...
Sharokh's for dinner!
Worrying little man.
Hairy bastard.

Must wake up in time.
8hours. 4pm
Perfect

Just lie here
Something will change eventually
Hellfire that is bright.
It's going to be a splendid day.

SHAHAB: So, sleep . . .

Shahab sleeps. As he sleeps he draws circles with his hand.

Leila has been sitting on a chair
Leila catches her breath. She listens. She is in the park.

LEILA: At lunch time I go to the park and listen to the birds.

Bird song. There is a sense that for an extended moment she is with them. That she is at home with them.
Breath.

Long beat

LEILA: In 4 hours time
I'll be on commuter the train again.

In 5 hours time
I'll be cycling home.
All weather jacket. Bike shorts. Helmet.

Beat

LEILA: This is me cycling home.

Leila describes with her hands, a rocket launching and a fuel pod falling back to earth as the command module flies into orbit. Her body follows the movement whilst her focus remains in the park.

SHAHAB: I have a recurring dream.
My family are the galaxy.
Dad is the sun and the rest of them, Mum, Parsa, Neda, Rasa and Sharock.
Grandparents, aunties, uncles, cousins.
All of them.
And everyone is there, but me.
I look and I look, but I am nowhere.
It is like someone has forgotten to draw me in.
And last night Anja was there.
Anja! Who is almost a stranger!

I try to get back to sleep.

In 4 hours time,
I will get up.
In 5 hours time
I'll be composing a poem for Anja as I'm driving to Sharok's

Beat

LEILA: This is me cycling home.

Beat

This is me driving to Sharoks.

Both the actors light a match and light sparklers that fade out as the music ends. Over Max Richer: Walk from the Rue Villin.

SCENE 3: HISTORIES

LX   *Warm bright state.*
Leila and Shahab greet the audience with direct eye contact and open heartedness. There is an intimacy and ease between them. It is the year 2021.

LEILA: I'm Leila

SHAHAB: I'm Shahab

They look at each other and share a moment. Then continue.

LEILA: This is me waiting for my mother when I am 5.
That's my Christmas dress I'm wearing, even though its March and mum didn't believe in Christmas.
Those long socks!
I was a worrying little girl.
I still do that clasping things with my hands.

SHAHAB: This is the hospital I was born in in Tehran in 1972
That area probably looks a lot different now.
It used to be quite an elegant part of town.
And that's my mother with me, the tiny speck.

Its 7 years before the revolution.

LEILA: Here's me, asleep in my dad's office at the Bell Foundry. That's my junior school uniform, so I must be about 8.
It was about that time my little sister Cecelia was born.
I have many memories of being driven home through London streets after dark. Lamps light flicking by overhead.

SHAHAB: This is one of the houses my father designed in Bug Sur California.
Its beautiful isn't it?
He had an excellent eye.
After my brother and sisters were born we moved there for eight years.
Dad didn't want to move back, but mum's whole family are in Iran, so...
My Dad is American by birth.

LEILA: This is Marty Smith.
My Dad worked for NASA in the 60s, thats where they met.
He came for dinner once when I was eleven.
Marty flew around the moon twice.
Twice!! He never landed.
He said he'd wanted to, but that he was

glad now because those guys had no end of trouble.
He was really great. He said with my brain I could do what I liked.

He's probably why I did Engineering...

SHAHAB: This is my Dad, visiting the Esalan Institute in California in 1969. Esalan was the centre of the human potential movement back then.
The man standing next to him is the Joseph Campbell... the mythologist and next to Joseph is my dad's hero, Buckminster Fuller.
It isn't that my father is short, but Joseph Campbell is tall.
Its funny, because to me, Dad was a giant. A god.
I always saw him like that.

LEILA: This is my mum, Esther, singing in her hey day.
When I was little my mother told me my name meant 'waiting' and that she chose it because when I finally did come, I was three weeks late.
She said I'd kept her waiting forever.
I used to think about that while I waited for mum out the front of pubs all over the

east end; Whitechapel,
Spitalfields,
Mile End.
It was my first understanding of irony.

SHAHAB: This is my extended family.
And this one
And this one
There are hundreds of them.
See me? I'm in just about every picture.
I was quite a show off.
That's my little brother Parsa.
Well, little!! He is now the father of three and turns 40 next year. 40!!
Parsa is about 13 here.

LEILA: This is me. In silhouette – no flash.
Its 2004 and mum had just died.
I was furious at her.
That she had wasted her life.
That she chose booze over us. Death over us.
That night, on a hunch, I looked up the meaning of my name,
It doesn't mean 'waiting' at all,
It means Night, or Darkness.

SHAHAB: This is my class at film school in London.
That's me third from the left at the front.
I had pretty bad hair back then.

I mean, that's bad. Isn't it?

Still, attraction never seemed to be the problem.

LEILA: This is me without my glasses. Angry. I was always so angry.
When I get angry, all I can hear is humming in my ears.
It is still like that.
Although these days I can feel it coming, like a storm.
I recognise the atmospheric conditions.
I can get everyone to clear out.

SHAHAB: This is back stage at the Culture show.
I had a small volume of poetry published a while back.
It got lots of attention after the London bombings in 2007.
I became a poster boy for a movement.
Like being a man from the middle east and writing love poetry made me special.
As if it hasn't been happening since the dawn of time.
He was a great interviewer and a lovely man.
We had a great conversation afterwards.
But he didn't get the book
He didn't get it at all.

LEILA: And I bought that book.
And it was signed too, so...

She pulls up another image

This is me working on one of the museum's temporary exhibits
Exhibitions isn't my usual department - I didn't normally have to wear a uniform.
It's pretty obvious that I wasn't enjoying myself.
That's the Iranian attache I'm standing next to and his party.
It was my job to greet them and show them around.
I overheard one of them say: 'look at that angry little attendant'.

SHAHAB: It wasn't me.

LEILA: It was.
He always says this.
Anyway.

SHAHAB: Anyway.

They riff/ tiff for a while. After the 4th 'Anyway', they begin again.

SHAHAB: This is Eugenia. Stylish. Educated. A bit

dull.
And Soraya.
And ahhhm Sophie? Sophia?
This is Tereza. Terez. French. A bit clingy.
She lasted maybe... a month I think.
Give or take.
And Nicole. Single mother. Outspoken.
Very English.
Nice.
Not right.
But nice.

I don't really have many pictures of the others...
Except for Anja...

SCENE 4

SHAHAB: *This* is Anja.

Leila becomes Anja. Shahab watches her from a distance. Remembering the night.

> Not my usual type.
> Golden. Delicate.
> Had a little boy.
> No husband. Well not at this point.
> She just arrived at my house one evening for writer's group
> And... it was like the quality of light suddenly changed.
> I couldn't stop watching her...
> She had a magnificent script, it silenced everybody.
> But it wasn't that...
>
> We fell in love.
>
> This day, was the day of the crash.
> It was also, my 40th birthday.

Shahab enters the scene. Anja has been reading at the table. He is warm and affectionate as lovers are. She is playful and flirtatious but a lot more reserved.

ANJA: Shabby, you told me it was a party.

SHAHAB: It is a party, but just for us.

He smiles conspiratorially.

ANJA: Ok.
You tricked me.

SHAHAB: I wanted you all to myself.

ANJA: Ahhh

She sighs

ANJA: I have a card for you
Happy Birthday.

He kisses her on the neck.
He ignores the card and goes back to the kind of attention he was giving her at the top of the scene.

SHAHAB: OK. Now, I can drive us to the airport in the morning
I've also.
Look...

He grabs her hand and pulls her to the doorway of the spare bedroom. She follows but her energy is going in the opposite direction. As she looks into the immaculately made up bedroom, she has a terrible sinking feeling that increases throughout the next bit of dialogue. Shahab is oblivious to it.

Anja looks completely confused.

SHAHAB: They can stay *here*.

ANJA: Who?

SHAHAB: Your parents.
For the whole week if they like.
There is so much more space here.
It really is no problem.

ANJA: Right...

SHAHAB: Iris can bring breakfast...
Or we could all eat out!
I had keys cut.

ANJA: Ohhh... uhmm.

SHAHAB: And Anja,

...I've been thinking...

ANJA: Yah...

SHAHAB: I would adore it if you...
I've put a lot of thought into this...
I would adore it if you would consider

being here with me all the time.

Would you? Anja?

ANJA: Ahhmm... ahhh.

SHAHAB: You have inspired me to love.
You are precisely not the kind of person I would ever normally feel this way about.
But I do.
You have me.
Anja?

ANJA: Ahh.
Woah.
Ahh... this is all
Thank you
But...

SHAHAB: Take some time
You don't have to decide now.
We've got all the time in the world.

ANJA: Ok.
Thank you.

SHAHAB: And you can use this room as an office.
You can write, read.
I can bring you...

ANJA: Shabby!
Its wonderful, but
I can't...
Its too much!

SHAHAB: What do you mean?

ANJA: You are lovely, Shabby, but your life is a fairy tale.

SHAHAB: Pardon me? *(genuinely taken aback)*

ANJA: No one lives like this.
Its not real!

SHAHAB: I don't know what you mean...

ANJA: I've met someone else.

You know him.
He's from our Monday group.

SHAHAB: Andrew.
Alexis
Clive?

Clive?!!!

Clive has a wife!

ANJA: He had a wife.

SHAHAB: He's too old for you!
He's dull!
He has no self-respect, can't even get his lunch into his mouth!

ANJA: Ha, yes. he's a bit of a mess.
But I quite like that
He makes me laugh.
He's a brilliant writer.

Sorry.

She puts her hand on his.

He takes his hand away and retracts his warmth like a snails antennae being touched

It was just a party all the time.
Did you really think it could last?

Scene fades. Anja becomes Leila again.

LEILA: Here's me saying goodbye to my sister at Heathrow.
That's Cecelia's husband Paul. He's a doctor. Clever guy.
Nice enough. A bit cold.

I was furious at her for leaving, but I didn't say.

Shahab becomes Julie. She is winding up cables from her glider and looking out over the Downs.

LEILA: This is Julie,
The hang-gliding instructor.
This was the day of the crash.
She was incredibly sporty.
I was supposed to take my first class with Julie,
She was only 25 years old, but already a veteran.
She was one of most confident, relaxed people I'd ever met.

Leila clings to the ground a few metres away from the edge of the cliff edge.

JULIE: Just come next Saturday and try again, I don't mind.

LEILA: Oh thank you, that's really generous. But I don't expect it.

JULIE: Look, people panic all the time. It is very common.
Its nothing to be embarrassed about.

LEILA: I've wanted to do it my whole life.

	I've just.
There's always been a million things I need to get done first.
And I've always thought, eventually one day.
But...
Anyway, Dad died last year, finally!
JULIE:	God! I'm sorry.
LEILA:	No its fine.
Really, its fine.
He was a grumpy old bastard at the end.
Not that he was a total arsehole,
He just didn't know what he was doing.
Anyway, I promised myself, I would do something about it when I had my time back. And now, you know, I've got my time back, so, you know, no more excuses.
But, I bloody get here, and I completely over think it. Get myself into a total state and. God! I mean, what the fuck I was thinking!!
Clearly I need my head read. Counselling or something. its not normal, is it?

Julie thinks for a moment and is about to speak when Leila continues.

I had a panic attack on a plane a few years ago.

As I was *getting* on a plane.

I was going to visit my sister, who lives in New Zealand.

Which is a ridiculous place to live anyway.

I mean who would live in New Zealand?

It was pretty bad.

British Airways won't let me fly with them anymore.

Sometimes even on flat ground it feels like I am on a slant.

Like we are all sliding into a pit.

I read somewhere that vertigo isn't the fear of falling, it is the desire to fall, but catching yourself.

She takes a breath in.

JULIE: So go with the desire; let the wing catch you.

LEILA: Fucking hell. Did you just hear yourself?!

JULIE: Just let go.
Take the risk.

Maybe try it without your glasses?

> Things'd be blurry, so you wouldn't have to see the edges of everything.

Metronomy's The Look fades up over the next passage. When the beat kicks in, the scene dissolves into the next one.

LEILA: Fucking hell.

JULIE: Look.
Come here.
Just take a step forward and look down over the cliff.
Its not that scary.
Come on.
I've got you. See? Its easy.
You ready?
OK, on the count of 3...
1, 2...

LEILA: No!

Leila goes into her shock/ denial as Julie dissolves into 2021 Shahab watching Leila in that state she was in. Then eventually dissolves back into Shahab at the time before the crash. They break off into their respective holding patterns. And go through denial, anger and convincing themselves they were on the wrong track with their quests. Lines begin slowly, while the characters return to their orbits. Then gradually they pick up tension / pace until Shahab is whirling and Leila is frenetic. Over the next text the music changes to sound like it is coming from a car radio.

LEILA: Never doing that again. What a terrible teacher. £200 on a stupid course!

SHAHAB: I don't live in a fairy tale...

LEILA: Why am I wasting my time on this madness?

SHAHAB: Clive is an idiot. What is she thinking?

LEILA: Got to organise Dad's things.

SHAHAB: I'm much funnier.

LEILA: Got to get Dad's house on the market.

SHAHAB: She wasn't worthy of me. I'm going to call Tereza.

LEILA: I've got so much to do!

SHAHAB: I'll go to Hotel Du Vin tonight. Pick up a waitress.

CRASH – full score –

Real time crash.

As per the opening but the characters have just come out of their rituals:
Shahab's radio playing Metronomy: The Look.
Step.
Impact!
Shahab is thrown back into his seat at the same time as Leila is hit by the bonnet of his car and thrown into the air. Both of them are still for an extended split second.

LX and SFX shift signifying change in Leila's conscious state. (Shahab stays in his chair/car)
Time slows down.
Ultra presence.
All other noise quietens.

From contraction, limb from limb is slowly dismembered from the body starting with the spine. Butoh style.
Each limb releasing corresponds with a thought. Eventually she is in flight, suspended in a sustained moment.

LEILA V/O: Oh, this is happening.
...Yes, this is definitely happening.
Shit. It cant happen yet!
Who's going to look after Dad? Oh he's dead.
I haven't been to Acapulco yet.
Look how far away the ground is.

Just before she lands, thoughts start water-falling out of her

> I won't get to see Mark turn one.
> I haven't owned my own home.
> I never even had a vaginal orgasm.

State change. She falls in real time.
There is a moment as consciousness leaves the body.
Then in voice over. Refrain of bird song.
The sound of the wind.

> It's Cecelia smiling at me kindly and handing me that air ticket.
> It's Marty Smith patting me on shoulder and telling me I should go out and grab life with both hands.
> It's my mother and I laughing and laughing because I'm making a huge mess of the cling film.

Leila dies.

Shahab sits still stunned. Eyes cast slightly down, but distant. He speaks as if completely matter of fact, but the body is telling a completely different story. Cold heart. Distant head. Spine moves, the rest falls away.
A slow beat begins. Low blood pressure. Like blood is drained from the heart.
SFX the noises of the crash continue, but in a muffled remote way, like they are coming through someone else's headphone.

SHAHAB: I drove off.

Beat
The body moves forward.
Beat.

       I parked.

Beat.
He doesn't move.
Beat.

       I got out of the car.

Beat.
He moves and stands with his back to Leila.
Beat.

       I walked.

Beat.
He walks. He walks right off stage in a disembodied and automatic way.
The beat accelerates and grows in volume, until it is clear that it is a heart beat.

Shahab comes briskly back on stage with a very different rhythm. There is an urgency and real anxiety.
He climbs the hill to get a vantage point and looks down at the dead body on the ground.
Suddenly we switch back to real time and the sound of the real world (ambulence, cars, voices etc) rushes back into his

experience. His body goes into trauma and he tries to breathe.

Leila leaves her dead body there and her spirit gets up to address the audience.
Both her and Shahab are looking at her dead body.

LEILA: 15 minutes.
I lost 15 minutes of living.
Later people would ask: were they full?
What were they full of.
And I would say mostly forgetting and silence and stillness.
Then suddenly this feeling that I was not yet done
That we were not yet done.

LEILA: *gasps*

SHAHAB: *sighs*

End of ACT I

ACT II

SCENE 1

Leila takes off her shoes and glasses

SHAHAB: After the ambulance left, I walked down to where she'd been.
People were just getting on with life as if nothing had happened!

Nobody saw me.
Perhaps I was invisible.
I expected someone to shout. 'He did it. It was him. I saw him drive off!!'
But nothing. Nothing at all.

Something bright and shining caught my eye, beside a drain.
It looked like tin foil.
I knew it was hers.
I'm not sure why. I just knew.

It was a necklace.
Not beautiful.
A pendant made of some unrecognisable material.
I picked it up.
And I didn't go to the hospital
I didn't collect the car.

I just walked home.

When I got there it didn't feel like home.
More like a shell I'd been rattling around in.

So I turned off all the lights.
And I sat
And looked out to sea.

LX reality shift.

SCENE 2

Mes by Merkof (or something similar)

Shahab in his home at night. He is still shivering a bit and smoking looking out to sea. Towards a more distant, more complicated home. SFX of the sea.

Leila is in a coma in her hospital bed.

Shahab makes a series of phone calls. Over the next passage, the last of the light is draining away from the horizon leaving a deep red line.
He calls his mother. His sister, his brother.
No one picks up.
He runs out of thoughts. He looks out to sea again.
He tries Anja.
Nothing.

The underworld of his fears start to wind themselves around his ankles pulling him down. As it does, the music begins to suck inward to a claustrophobic muffledness. Alchemical monsters. Orobourous and demons. Spinning dervishes and orbits off axis.

Shahab is pulled backwards in spite of himself almost through time and space into the hospital room. Shahab looks at Leila and tries to work out how to be.

Meanwhile Leila's table glows softly

LX shift.

SHAHAB: Uhhm... hello.
I don't know what I'm doing here.
I'm your cousin. If they ask.

He can't think of anything else to say.
He looks at her for a prolonged moment until he starts to feel a bit uncomfortable.
He looks around for stimulus material. Finds a Hello! magazine.

Gorgeous George!
Kate and Wills invite us into the royal nursery!
Do you read this stuff?

Kate looks radiant in a fuschia wraparound dress!
Baby George, *(he looks at her)* you'll be pleased to know, is sleeping soundly!

Hmmm
Err Vanish Oxyaction Crystal White Powder gets great results even at 30 degrees.
...it also says here.

He puts the magazine down. Looks at her again.

Has another prolonged moment of 'what the fuck am I doing here?'

>Blueberry?
>They've been washed.
>I could ask if they'd mash it up and feed it into your drip, if you like.
>
>That was a joke.
>
>I'm just going to get something from the cafeteria.

He gets up

>Want anything?
>
>...I'll ahh.
>I'll come back...

LX shift. Down on Shahab. Fade up in a way that emphasises Leila and the suggestion of an altered state for her. Fade back up of Sun Harmonics by John Hopkins.

LEILA V/O: Kate? Who is Kate?
Well she can't put fuschia in with Vanish, she'll never get that colour back.
Half a scoop. Tell her no more than half a scoop.
Someone needs to tell her.

Has he gone to tell her?
Who?
Oh I'm the person who goes.
I'll go. Legs?
Come on legs! What's wrong with you?

Leila's toes twitch and a muscle twinges in her right leg. The body begins very very gradually, to wake up. Nervous system twitches, electrical impulses waking up. Into slow breathed extensions / fluid body undulations. Into recovery / rest.

Music tapers down slightly as Shahab 're-enters' the bedside reality.
Lx shift to reflect this.

SHAHAB: Right. Today is poetry
Fallen asleep already?!
No, this stuff is good.
You'll love this.
Hafiz:
'Everyone
Is god speaking.
Why not be polite
And listen to him.'

Oh...
(he turns the page to see if there's more. There's not)
Some of them are quite short.

Leila's score continues. He sits in silence for a moment reading to himself. He finds another one. Leila

   OK here's one.
   'It is all just a love contest
   And I never lose.
   Now you have another good reason to spend more time with me.'

He chuckles to himself.

Eventually looks for something else to do/say.

SHAHAB: Do you think that Nigerian nurse fancies me?
   She keeps bringing me tea

   If you can call it tea.
   Ha!

   The toilets here are dreadful, by the way
   My kingdom for a catheter!
   Some people have all the luck.

   ...it is disconcerting that you don't... laugh at my jokes.

   So... do you have any relatives, or am I really it?
   Not joking now: Where are your relatives?

There can't be none.
No one has *none*.

Did you do something unspeakable to them?

I usually turn left. But for some reason I didn't that day.
Had some woman in my head.
It was my fortieth birthday. Did you know that?

Oh, I have this.
(he pulls out the necklace)
It's yours isn't it?
(he looks at it)
I don't know what to do with it.

What is it made of... by the way?

I'll keep it.
Its safe.
Don't worry.

LEILA V/O: Something's not right. Something's not.
The pieces aren't fitting together.
Something's missing.

There's Dad on the Brooklyn Bridge with a woman on his arm.

Mum! God its Mum! Mum, you were so beautiful!
All my relatives.
Did I do something unspeakable?
A lounge-room. Everything is orange... is it night?
Yes. There's my Dad sitting on the sofa. He used to have so much more hair.
His face is flickering. Watching rockets launching on a black and white television
There mum passed out on his lap.
No me yet.
Or maybe.
Yes! I am there.
Just a few cells.
Now I'm moving through a tunnel
I am a single cell whizzing through a blood red tunnel.
Now I am just a thought.
Now I am the space before thought.

There's a boat. They're on a boat
There's a green statue
And queueing. Hours and hours of queueing.
Tired, skinny people.
There's my grandma! She is so fragile!!
Its New York city...
But a long time ago.

> Now there are thousands of people dressed in black
> A desert. They are wandering across a desert.
> Their clothing flaps like crows wings or...
> Now they are becoming lizards and birds.
> Ancient black shining creatures.
> Flapping and slithering.
> Flapping, slithering, cawling, chattering.
>
> What a terrible racket!!
> We are sleeping. Can't you see??!!!
> How rude!!

LX shift.
Fade back up of Sun Harmonics by John Hopkins. Down on Shahab. Fade up in a way that emphasises Leila and the suggestion of an altered state for her. Leila's stomach, spine begins to come to life. Head is still dead. Nervous system twitches, electrical impulses waking up. Into slow breathed extensions / fluid body undulations. Into recovery / rest.
This continues over Shahab's next bit.
He says it as if he's talking to her head. Sometimes he seems to be talking to himself.

SHAHAB: *(reads from a book again)*
'He sat alone in space as a cloud that floats in nothingness.
He slept not, for there was no sleep:

He hungered not for as yet there was no hunger.'

...actually I am quite hungry...

'So he remained for a great while, until a thought came to his mind.
He said to himself 'I will make a thing'.'

Hmmm.

So, that's a myth from the Gilbert Islands.
Its Carl Sagan again. Cosmos.
Did you see it?
Interesting...

Ahhh....
Spoke to my mother last night.
Didn't tell her about you.

I mean, what would I say?

I felt I should
It's the first time I've spoken to her since...

Shahab looks at her. He reaches out and strokes her forehead and hair. There is tenderness in it. And the next passage is delivered with an intimacy he hasn't allowed before.

I'm stuck. I've never been stuck.

I can't move.

I just come here...
That's all I do.

It is.
Actually. All I do.
I can't...
Do anything else...

LX shift. Down on Shahab. Fade up in a way that emphasises Leila and the suggestion of an altered state for her. Fade back up of Sun Harmonics by John Hopkins. Fade up in a way that emphasises Leila and the suggestion of an altered state for her. The shoulder begins to wake up. Then the hip. Into hands legs. She tries to stand. Head is still dead. Nervous system twitches, electrical impulses waking up. Into slow breathed extensions / fluid body undulations. Into recovery / rest.
This continues over Shahab's next bit until she is standing up on the bed. Her arms begin ti float upwards. She becomes an eagle. She takes flight. Her eyes open. She notices something pulling her attention to the right of her.

LEILA V/O: There's been an accident.
Is somebody hurt?
Somebody has to do something.
Where is everyone?
Can you go and get everyone please.
You're not listening!

Where's he gone?
There's been an accident!
Someone's crashed their car into a bicycle!
There's a woman in the air!
Look!
Why can't anyone see?!
I recognise her.
She has the same shoes as...
Oh fuck. It's me!
It's me in the air!
I'm flying.
My god.
Breathe! Remember to breathe!
Just let go. Take the risk!
(She breathes)
Wonderful!
My God. Its wonderful!
Who's that person to my right?
Who's there?
Who are you?
Why do you keep turning away?
Show me your face!

As Leila sits, she turns to look at the place where her head was.
Fade down / up
Watches her again.

SHAHAB: I can't do this anymore.

You're taking up all my time.

I can't sleep.

You're not going to wake up, are you?

You're pretty much dead.
I'm wasting my life away visiting a fucking dead person.

I don't even know who you are.

You don't belong to anyone.

Who are you?!

This is insane.

I've got to get on with things...
I've got to go.

He gets up. He looks at her one last time.

She is somehow lighter, very much awake. Leila switches off all the lights and leaves.

END ACT II

ACT III

SCENE 1

Sound score: Neil De Grasse Tyson speaking about us in the universe and the universe in us underscored by the Cinematic Orchestra's 'To Build a Home (or something similar). Movement score describing Leila and Shahab's unstable make-ups trying to evolve / rebalance themselves. Spirals moving towards each other into a tight centre into spinning. Into neutral. Then very gradually into reverse: L grows towards air / light, S grows towards earth

SCENE 2

Lights up on Shahab who is alone in his vast apartment, now packed up and ready for moving except for a table and a chair. He is down stage in the far corner, trying to work out the instructions on the side of a jar of pain killers. Shahab listens to Degrasse Tyson / to Build a Home on his headphones. His front door buzzes. He takes his earphones out as the sound fades out. He buzzes the person in and leaves the door ajar without looking. Beat.
Leila stands in the door way. She is weighed down with shopping bags.

SHAHAB: Gosh.

Well... Hello.

LEILA: Did you run me over with your car?

...

Did you?

SHAHAB: You didn't look.

LEILA: No.

I was panicking.

I remember you.
I remembered your voice.

In the queue just now. Your accent.
Something about the back of your head.

SHAHAB: You were in the supermarket?

LEILA: Aha.

SHAHAB: Uhm.
You can put your bags down.

They look at each other. Like different species in the zoo.

There's food being delivered.
Would you like wine?

LEILA: I don't drink wine.

SHAHAB: Uhm. I may have the ingredients for a martini.

LEILA: Ha. I don't drink.
At all.

SHAHAB: Did you follow me?

LEILA: Yep

Silence. They stare at each other.

LEILA: Is this a ball room?

SHAHAB: Yes.
Used to be.

LEILA: Fucking hell.
Where's all your furniture?

SHAHAB: Packed up.

I'm moving...

LEILA: Right.

Silence. Leila stares at him, wondering where to start. he avoids her gaze.

I've got your book of poetry. You're a poet?

SHAHAB: No. I'm a film maker.

LEILA: What films have you made?

SHAHAB: None as yet.

LEILA: You're not really a film maker then are you?

Silence. They look.

SHAHAB: And you? What do you do?

LEILA:	Uhm, nothing at the moment. I used to work in a museum. But that was... I don't anymore.
SHAHAB:	Why not?
LEILA:	I got hit by a car.
SHAHAB:	How much do you want?
LEILA:	What?
SHAHAB:	Would you accept 200?
LEILA:	I don't understand.
SHAHAB:	£200,000, would that do? That's is why you've come isn't it?
LEILA:	No! No, actually.
SHAHAB:	Then why are you here?
LEILA:	Uhm I don't know. I saw you in Waitrose.

I remembered your voice.
It was your voice mostly.

Did you come and read to me in hospital?
The nurse said someone came almost everyday.

SHAHAB: Yes.

LEILA: Why?

And then you stopped.

SHAHAB: Yes.

LEILA: Why?

SHAHAB: It gets depressing. Talking to a dead person.

LEILA: I wasn't dead.

SHAHAB: Might as well have been.

LEILA: You're being quite cold.
I don't remember you cold.
You seemed funnier.
Kinder...

SHAHAB: ...Sorry.

Its not...

Its not a situation I'm used to dealing with.

Got used to you not answering back.

LEILA: Ha.

SHAHAB: Could you hear me?

LEILA: Not really.

I knew stuff was going on.
I just couldn't make sense of it.
I knew you were there. Well, that someone was there.
I knew I was trapped.
Sometimes you looked like my father and other people I know.
Once you were a talking snake trying to eat its own tail.
Once you were The Duchess of Cambridge Advising me on cleaning products.
I couldn't work anything out.

Then I remembered I had seen you.

SHAHAB: When?

LEILA:	Just now in the queue.
	I finally remembered I had seen you through your windscreen. From the bonnet of your car. I'd forgotten that. It came back.

Shahab feels the blood drain away from his head.

	Do you remember seeing me?
SHAHAB:	Yes. Yes I do.
LEILA:	(*She looks at him sensing he is hiding a lot.*)
	I found your book, last week as I was packing up Dad's flat, I bought it, years ago. There's a photo of you on the back.
SHAHAB:	Oh that dreadful photograph.
LEILA:	You had quite... big hair...
SHAHAB:	Yeah, I wanted to kill my press agent for using that one.
LEILA:	You're American.

SHAHAB: No. Yes.
I'm Iranian.
Iranian / American.
British
I'm from everywhere.

LEILA: In the coma, I thought I was in America.
I thought, 'I can't remember moving here!!'
'Have I been kidnapped?!'
I thought 'that's why no one can find me!'

I remembered so many odd and specific things.
The look on this woman's face as she watched me in the air. Just horror.
I remembered noticing bird song. In surround sound.

Your face.
I even remembered your car.

Bits of the past came back.
Bits of flight.

Remembering how to fly.
It is ancestral, that memory.

Why did you come?
You didn't have to.

SHAHAB: Yes I did.

LEILA: Why?

SHAHAB: You didn't have anyone else.

LEILA: ...Yes I did.
My sister.

Although she was hard to track down.

SHAHAB: Why?

LEILA: Well her last name has changed. She's Cecilia Silvestre.
Plus she's in my phone as 'Kiwi Traitor'.
Might not have helped.

She arrived in the fifth week, just as I was coming out of it. - Great!
She was pissed off at *me* for not getting in touch!

Anyway.

So.
You drove off.

SHAHAB: I did.

LEILA: You seem pretty cool about that.

SHAHAB: I'm not.

>I had a bit of hash in my pocket. Was worried there might be police...

LEILA: That's *it*?!
God, you must feel *terrible*!

Shahab attempts to take in her response.
Pause.
The door bell goes.

SHAHAB: That's the food.
Please stay for supper.

LEILA: No thanks.
I think that might feel weird.

She collects her bags of shopping. She has another good look at him.

>Maybe I shouldn't have come.
>I thought you'd be...
>I don't know.
>Different.

SHAHAB: Please stay.
Sorry.

Please?
It would mean a lot.

She puts down her shopping bags. Lights Fade.

SCENE 3

Later that night. Fade up on Leila and Shahab just finishing their food.

LEILA: Where are you moving to?

SHAHAB: Home.
Selling this place.
Going back to Iran.

LEILA: Is that a good thing?

SHAHAB: I don't know.
I have no idea.
You ask a lot of questions.
It's a complicated place. Beautiful. Difficult.

LEILA: You know that thing, 'if you're stuck, move'?
Just move, in *a* direction.
Any direction.
You'll quickly realise if it is the wrong direction.
You know?

SHAHAB: Yeah, right.
Well I guess I'm doing that.
I'm going to try moving backwards.

See if I can... work a few things out.

LEILA: Thanks for dinner.

SHAHAB: My pleasure.

LEILA: That was...
Well that was alright wasn't it?

SHAHAB: Yes.

LEILA: Ok.
Well, I should probably be going.

SHAHAB: Really?

LEILA: Its quite late,
I should be job hunting in the morning.

SHAHAB: Don't go.

LEILA: Ahhhm.

SHAHAB: Please don't.

Sorry. Go if you need to.
Of course!
Haha. I'll call you a cab...
I'm just enjoying your company.
Its helping.

Having you here.
Talking to you.

It helps.

LEILA: ...
Ok.
For a little bit.

God I'm never going back.

Can't.
Got no idea what's next.
But its definitely not backwards.
What about America?
Can't you go to America?
They make a lot of films over there.

SHAHAB: There's no family. I'd be starting from scratch. No point.

Leila thinks about this.

LEILA: So why England?

SHAHAB: Came to study. Film school. Never went back.

LEILA: And never made films.

SHAHAB: Yeah ok.

LEILA: ...Well its true.

I trained as an engineer.
Aeronautical Engineering,
That was my passion I guess.
Never done it.
Somehow I ended up in an office under the earth doing god knows what.

My Dad worked for NASA

SHAHAB: Oh.

LEILA: He was a professor of metalurgy. developed alloys.
Heat resistant metals for space flight.
So... Aeronautics.
Not a huge leap.

Silence. They look. Something occurs to Shahab. He crosses the space to a box on the mantle piece. Collects Leila's necklace.

SHAHAB: I have this.
Its yours isn't it?

LEILA: Oh wow. Yes.
Thought I'd lost that.

SHAHAB: What is it made of?

LEILA: Its a titanium alloy.
From Dad.
Its a key ingredient in rocket fuselages.

SHAHAB: Rocket fuselages...
Is it valuable?

LEILA: Sort of.

SHAHAB: What do you mean?

LEILA: Well it has a very high tensile strength.
Even at extreme temperatures.
It is also powerfully corrosion resistant...
Titanium is one of the most heat resistant pure metals,
But alloyed, it is like a super power.
Problem is, it is - or was - a very difficult element to work with.

SHAHAB: Why?

LEILA: Well, it melts at an extremely high temperature.
1668 degrees to be exact.
So blending it with other metals until fairly recently, the 60's, 70's, was thought impossible.

Even now, the technology for smelting is vertiginously expensive.
The ore is actually not that uncommon, raw...

Sorry, is this boring?

SHAHAB: No, not at all!
Please!

LEILA: The Russians had so much more titanium in their soil, their smelting technologies for were ahead of NASA during the space race.
They were used to working with it you see.
So we had to play catch up.
That's why they approached Dad.
This is Dad's first attempt at the alloy that became Aerospace Grade 5
Its the most famous of Titaniums.
It is still considered an optimum material in certain aspects of rocket manufacture.
And these days it is used to make high end jewellery and trinkets etcetera,
This is *the* first sample.

SHAHAB: Right.
Right.
Wow.
So you're following in your Dad's footsteps.

LEILA: Ha.
My Dad was some kind of alchemist really.
No one knows how he did what he did.

I've been having some ideas,
I've been working on some designs for using solar power
It's the next big thing in commercial air travel.
Obviously.

Shahab has been watching her. He laughs

LEILA: What?

SHAHAB: Just your language: 'Obviously'.
Not obvious at all!

He takes a moment to really look at her.

You shine when you speak about all this.

You're luminous.

LEILA: Hmm...

SHAHAB: You're shy!

LEILA: It isn't special this stuff.

SHAHAB: Yes it is.
You're amazing.

Leila hears what he says but doesn't know how to receive it.

SHAHAB: Don't worry. I didn't mean...

LEILA: Sorry.
I don't know what to say to that. I don't know what...
People don't...

SHAHAB: Hey, its ok.

LEILA: ...
Why did you come to the hospital really?
You felt guilty.

SHAHAB: No.

He thinks about it for a bit.

No... I felt...
I felt scared I guess.
It was a huge shock.
I was trying to make it real for myself ...or something.

It wouldn't let me be.

>   I still see your face through my windscreen
>   most night as I go to sleep...

LEILA: God! It's been a year!

SHAHAB: Yeah.
...yep. It has.

They look each other again.

Pause. A sense of time moving around them and the space between them being the still point of the turning world.

She smiles at him. Lights down.

SCENE 4

Later that night/ following morning. Lights up.
They sit on the roof terrace. It is 5am and they have been awake all night, talking. Shahab has dozed off for a few hours in his chair. Leila 'has found pen and paper and is sketching some ideas. She draws for a while. Notices Shahab's spliff in the ash tray. She looks at him sleeping. Takes it to her lips. Lights it. Coughs and splutters. Puts it down again. Shahab wakes up.

LEILA: Sorry. Didn't mean to wake you.

Shahab smiles.

SHAHAB: That's ok.
You're still here.

LEILA: Yes.

She catches his gaze and looks away to her drawings.

Look, daylight.

SHAHAB: You sure you don't want the rest of this?

LEILA: I tried it. Its horrible.

He laughs

SHAHAB: You get over that. Work through it.

LEILA: This is an amazing place.
You are so lucky.
If I lived here, I'd want to spend everyday just looking out to sea.
I'd put my desk just there. And work in the sunshine.

SHAHAB: I asked someone to move in with me once.

LEILA: And she said no?

SHAHAB: Well she wasn't in love with me.

The truth is, I am not irresistible!

Leila laughs. They both laugh a little.

LEILA: You're funny.

SHAHAB: What's that? *(He points at her drawings)*

LEILA: Oh. I don't know.

SHAHAB: Looks like something from Minority Report.

LEILA: Hmmmm.
I'm working on an idea.

	I'll let you know when I work it out.
SHAHAB:	I guess I needed to get to the bottom of something.
LEILA:	What do you mean?
SHAHAB:	Why I came to the hospital.
	I needed to work something out.
LEILA:	And did you?
SHAHAB:	No. I will in Iran.
LEILA:	Right.
	You know, I can't see why this isn't easily transferrable.
	Commercial space flight is already happening. It's just a matter of time...

Shahab laughs.

LEILA:	What?
SHAHAB:	You're funny.

LEILA: I'm serious.

SHAHAB: I know. I like it.

LEILA: But it makes sense doesn't it?
It's just about finding the right materials.
And everything opening up at the right time.
That's it. That's all it is, really.

SHAHAB: I still don't know what you're talking about,
But I like you, so I'm going to nod and be encouraging.

Leila is focused on her work. Shahab is looking at Leila with new eyes.

LEILA: Isn't it funny how you look and look and when it finally comes the answer is simple. Like its been sitting there the whole time, waiting for you to find it.

SHAHAB: Yes.

Shahab is touched by metaphor. He is struck by the desire to speak a million things. He feels tears swelling up suddenly from a place he remembers vaguely, but doesn't understand. He reaches over and holds her hand. His heart is gripped by gratitude.

Thank you for staying with me last night.

Leila smiles

LEILA: That's ok.

I was going to sneak out, but I kept having ideas.

Are you ok?

SHAHAB: Yes.
Yes, I think I am.

I've spent over half my life here. Half!

Why have I put myself all the way over here?

On the other side of the world from everyone.
Everyone I love.

Why do I keep running away from everything?
All the connections I could be making
All the wonderful people I could be sharing my life with.
Here or there.

He looks into her.

I've been neither here nor there then!!

Love.
I've got to stop running away from love!

She puts her arms around him. Embraces him. He eventually allows it to warm him and open him
Lights fade.

SCENE 5

Lights up on the Histories state.
Leila and Shahab are delivering the next slides together rather than on opposite sides of the stage.

SHAHAB: This is Leila with her research team. She'd just received her first lot of funding to develop solar powered space flight. That was a couple of years ago, wasn't it?

LEILA: Yes last year. 2019.

SHAHAB: If it all goes to plan, she'll be launching her first prototype probe in 2032.
Also, the company have invited her to guest on the next commercial mission.

LEILA: Which is a huge privilege.

This is Shahab's house in Highbury in London.
That's his wife Mina there on the front steps.
You got married in Iran, that was an amazing day?

SHAHAB: Yes that was 2016. And then we moved back here after we had Mohsen.
The government is changing, but, I needed

                        to get my films made,
                        So Europe is easier.
                        We visit. A lot.

LEILA: And do you recognise the architecture? It was one of Shahab's Dad's designs?

SHAHAB: That's right. We wanted to make some kind of homage to him
                        And Mina is an architect, so.

LEILA: Oh this is just yesterday in a cafe in London.

SHAHAB: Cafe Florentine.

LEILA: Us and Mohsen.
                        I hadn't seen you for a while.

SHAHAB: How long had it been?

LEILA: Six months.

Lights shift into warm wash.

SCENE 6

SHAHAB: So, Venice have asked me to be on the panel discussion with Kiarostami. Kiarostami!

LEILA: Brilliant.

SHAHAB: I've never met him before. Been a fan my whole life... So... *(to Mohsen)* we're having a little holiday together, aren't we?

LEILA: How old are you now, Mohsen?

(Mohsen: I'm 4 and a 1/2)

Wow. 4 and a half! That's big!

(M: I know. How old are you?)

LEILA: I'm 46.

(M: are you as old as Dad?)

SHAHAB: Yes more or less the same age, aren't we? Give or take a year or two.

LEILA: What is that you're drawing?

(Mohsen: A rocket)

SHAHAB: Did you know Leila's Dad used to help build rockets?

(Mohsen: Did he? Wow. Did he go to the moon?)

SHAHAB: No, he didn't go to the moon.

LEILA: But I met someone who almost did once.
He flew around and around, but didn't land.

(Mohsen: Was he like Superman?)

LEILA: No, not like Superman.
More ordinary really. Like you and me.

I'm going into space next week.

*(Mohsen stares at her in awe.
M: Wow. Can I come?)*

SHAHAB: Haha.
Maybe. If you finish your salad.
You have to finish school first.
And do a few other things.

(Mohsen considers this.
M: Are you visiting another galaxy?)

LEILA: No, we'll only have time to visit our own galaxy.
We still haven't worked out a way to fly that fast.
We don't know if our bodies can cope with being away from earth for that long.

I'll show you. Look.
(*Leila draws a map of the solar system into the air in front of her.*)
This is Mars.
This is Venus.
And we are going all the way over here.
And when we get there, Earth will just be a tiny dot. See?
Like this.
And I'll be millions of miles away
I'll be looking back at all of you.
You and your Mum and Dad and all the other people we know.
And you'll be there, going to school and doing all the things you normally do.
And I'll be all the way over here.
Missing you and thinking about you, because you are so far away.

SHAHAB: But you'll be in here.

(*Shahab touches his chest.*)
All the time.
Where ever Leila is.
You'll always be here.

LEILA: And I'll be thinking, when can I see Mohsen again?
I have so much to tell him.

END